Poetic Rantings- A Collection of Emotional Outbursts from a Grumpy and Neurotic Human

Luke Mayo

BookLeaf Publishing

India | USA | UK

Presentation by *BookLeaf Publishing*

Web: www.bookleafpub.com

E-mail: info@bookleafpub.com

ISBN: 9789358736359

First edition 2023

*This book is dedicated to its readers,
whomever they may be. May you conquer
your emotional demons and find peace.*

ACKNOWLEDGEMENT

My powerful emotions have sometimes made me a difficult person to be around. There are many people in my life who have endured me, put up with me, helped me to manage myself, and loved me in spite of my emotional demons. As a result of this, not only have I lived a better life and become a better person, but I've been able to turn these situations into the creative writing you see written here.

These people deserve some thanks and acknowledgement, so here it is.

My colleagues in the various organisations I've worked and volunteered with, who have supported me in trying out new projects. My various classmates and faculty at University of Suffolk, who have helped me to realise and pursue my creative dreams. The team of counsellors at Renew Counselling, who have helped me through some of my darkest emotional times.

Most of all, my family, who have been constantly and permanently by my side through the best and worst times in my life. All of these groups, to a person, are in some way instrumental to making my life better, and making me better.

From the bottom of my heart: I love you all.

PREFACE

Humans are an emotional lot.

A testament to our humanity is our ability to feel emotions and be affected by them. Love, anger, sorrow, fear, hope, joy- it's all there, in the mix.

This book is a series of my own emotional responses to all kinds of things in life. Things that confuse me, things that upset me, things that annoy me, things that amuse me. Documenting and processing these matters in creative writing is what helps me embrace my life and humanity.

We can't stop or inhibit our emotions, nor should we. They are there to be felt and dealt with as best as possible. This book is my way of feeling and dealing with my emotions. I wish you, the reader, the best of luck in finding your own way to do the same thing.

The Price Isn't Right

There was once a time
Humans hunted for meat
Braving the elements
Facing mammoths, tigers and bears

Today
We hunt for money
Fending off a million debtors

Every meal we eat
Every shelter we reside
Every app we download
A price is attached

How high that price is

We once built empires
We once went to space
We once won wars

Now look at us
Broken and destroyed by money

Sleepless nights
Nervous breakdowns

Eviction notices
Tax receipts

We all owe money
Who to?
No name
No face
Just a silent and unremitting presence
Squeezing us dry

Money broke the system
How will we fix it?

Historical Hysteria

History
A subject once we learned from
Now we ignore it
Erase it
Rewrite it

There were vile characters
Awful situations
Horrifying chapters in the story of humanity

We used to remember them
Educate ourselves on them
Find ways to do better
Forge ahead to greater tomorrows

Now we're obsessed with what happened before
We're obsessed with pretending it didn't happen
We're obsessed with pretending people weren't
flawed
We're obsessed with deleting their existence if
they were

Objective history
True history
Honest history

Useful history
Real history

In this day and age
They're now history

Untimely Time

Something we can rely on
Time is the same for us all
It does not discriminate
It treats us alike

Months and years
Days and weeks
Hours and minutes

They pass at the same rate for us all

Those goals in life
The one we delay
The time they come varies
The common denominator?
They pass eventually

Will you be ready for yours?
Are you taking time seriously?
Are you letting it go?

Time passes exactly the same for us all
The way we use it is different for us all

Make time work for you

Harness its gifts to make hopes real

Time is untimely if you waste it
If you use it well it's a blessing

The Curse of Interruptions

Like pebbles hurled at me
Like cars swerving on the road
Like a digital screen stuck in a glitch

This is my train of thought

I just want to get on with life
Do what I need to do
Say what's on my mind

Housework
Jobs
Social life
Family
So many things to manage

Riddled with curveballs

"What was I going to say?"
Empty silence
"I'll just do the washing up"
The telephone rings
"I'll send you an email"
Computer shutdown

So many interruptions
So many curses
I don't want to interrupt the interruptions
I want them to stop

The No Job Centre

Another day of unemployment
Treading the barren wasteland of the job market

One the ironies of our time
Enormous pressure to get a job
No jobs to get

Fortnightly trips to the job centre
A vital part of the job hunt
Although I'm not sure why

I don't even know why they call it a job centre
You only get a job if you happen to work there

Humiliated when you attend
Punished when you don't attend
All for no reward
For the jobs never come

A futureless future
No job
No purpose
No change
No hope

This is our world

Weathering the Weather

Welcome to England
Enjoy your stay

Your options are as follows
Days of searing heat
Weeks of bitter cold
Months of sodden rain

Good luck guessing which one you'll get

From autumn through to spring
Gusts of wind
Clouds of storm
Wailing and weeping
On and on and on

Except for one week of summer

Rain pauses
Clouds part
Sunshine emerges
More than that
It burns

A scorched earth

A burnt population
Complete catatonia
Unable to handle the sun's rays

Then the week ends
So soon is the heatwave forgotten
Back we go to cold, wet, unremitting misery

The ongoing attempt to weather the weather

Imprisoned with Company

A restaurant meal
Doing my shopping
Going for a walk
A day out somewhere new

All by myself
How lovely
So peaceful

"You look lonely"
"Why are you on your own?"
"Being alone is sad"
"I'll join you"

Why?
Why are we doing this?
Why are we having this conversation?
Why are you judging my solitude?
Why are you forcing company onto me?

Why can't I be left alone?

I like myself
I respect myself
I'm ok on my own

Some times I prefer it

Don't presume to know my struggles
Don't pretend to be a hero
Don't force me to be saved from something not
real

I tell you I'm ok
I mean it
Spare me your pity
Save it for someone whose problems are genuine

There are problems in the world
Me being alone is not one of them
Imprisoning me in company is

Snobby Jobbies

Respect for your job
It comes at a price
Literally

Endless noughts on the end of your salary
A suit so sharp it can slice and dice a salad
Calling shots
The life of the big shots

They are important jobs
There are many more

Mops
Tills
Scaffolds
Power tools

Wield of one of these
There's no lack of importance
Just a lack of glitz and glamour

Your salary's lucky to have double digits
Never mind multiple zeroes
No pinstripes on your attire
Just a name badge

Shots called? No chance
Shots fired? So it would seem

The order of society
It puts these people at the bottom
The order of life
It falls apart without them

Remember this
When you forget your worth
Remember this
When other people ignore your worth
Remember this
When your worth is questioned or denied

No place for snobs in jobs

Distaste in Gorefests

Turning on the TV
Immediate chaos
Gunshots and bloodshed
People screaming
Anger and fear
Dismemberment of body and soul

Seeing it on the news is bad enough
Seeing it portrayed in fictional entertainment is
hell

For horror
For drama
For comedy
For public consumption

Why are we consuming it?

Limb-from-limb brutality
Blood and organs within forcibly moved without
Agony beyond any imagining
It's coming to a screen near you

Why do we do this in reality?
Why do we want to see this in fiction?

Surely we want to escape the torment?
How does seeing it in other people help?

Celebrations of gore
Not entirely to my taste

A Woman's Daring Escape

She's been immobile since forever
Ensnared by constructs forged by society
She is set in stone to be observed
But never loved

The sands of time are changing
Her manacles bind her no more
She challenges her captors
She no longer accepts the cards she's dealt

Subjugated by a fragile patriarchy
Basing its identity in control
She was a prime candidate for victimhood

A narrative written by male dominance
Nobody thought to change it
Everyone assumed this was ok
History took its course thus

Then she took a moment to think for herself
That's when the balance tipped in her favour
In the present moment she determines the future
for herself

Fate has been handed to her

No longer does she take it
For fate is hers to create

She is woman
She is individual
As worthy and capable as any other

Vibes of Autumn

Summer says goodnight
Rays of heat pack up and leave
Our days in the sun fade into nostalgia

While summer sleeps
Autumn awakes
Midday brightness morphs into a cool evening
breeze
Mellow sunsets adorn the sky
Lush yellows and greens become golden browns

Sensory pleasures
Apples and marshmallows
The crinch-crunch of leaves

Bonfires warm our hearts
Then our hearts are chilled by spooky tales
Whatever fears lurk ahead
We can keep each other safe

Remembrance of the dead
Respect for our forebears
Honour for their achievements
Continuing their legacy

Welcome to autumn
My favourite vibe of the year

Don't Need Changing

I once shuffled the back alleys of shame
Feeling the cold glares of judgement on me
The whispers of dislike surrounded me
The screams of hatred bellowed within me

No longer is this the route I take
I walk a different path
For I am a different person

I learned to identify the things I love
I learned to embrace them
I learned to become them

Now I walk the streets of joy
Head held high and smile worn wide
No whispers around me steal my attention
The only voice I heed is mine
It says "I love you"

The world tried to change me
I changed myself
The result is good

A Chance Encounter

Well here we are
I wasn't expecting to see you again
I wasn't expecting to see you at all
Not since you left

By the way
I've still got your jacket

You still have my innocence
My trust in people
My hopefulness

But you didn't get my fighting spirit
My will to live
They're still mine
And they always will be

I'll let you go
But I'll never let myself go

You won't see me again
You'll see the better me
The evolved me
The me you never had the chance to destroy
The me who jumps over hurdles

The me who climbs higher

It was nice where we were
It'll be better where I'm going

My Sleeping Needs

The joyful escapism which sleep brings
Simple and complicated
Easy and natural for some of us
A waking, sleeping nightmare for the rest

Where the lucky ones just do it
I need a routine
A process
A series of conditions and habits
Otherwise it's not to be

An abandonment of technology screens
My eyes and brain need no blue light
When the invisible waves transmit and vaporise
towards me
My brain has no hope of recovery

Instead
I replace the screens with pages
Choices of beloved reading material
Engaging the brain with distractions from reality
This is what helps me find restfulness

A comfortable place
An optimum temperature

Fabrics of reassuring material
The combination of winning sleep

This is what does it for me
Whatever works for you
Make sure you do it

Blessings of Anonymity

Watching the news
Reading the papers
Sometimes I wish I didn't

Festering cesspits of poison

Families royally at war
Politicians being slammed for all they do
New predatory revelations every day
Bad to read
Worse to live through

We have our problems
Job worries
Familial tension
Money strife
Health concerns

At least we don't have an audience watching

Imagine
Your next breakdown
Tears pouring
Sobs rupturing your throat
Your inner light and warmth extinguished

Then you turn and see it all
Flashing cameras
Journos salivating like hyenas
A world primed to dissect and judge you

Thank goodness this isn't you

The Power of Silence

The world's most powerful weapon
Ruining lives
Destroying civilisations
Getting worse the further it goes

No need for guns or bombs
Just use silence

Victims of evil
Bullying
Extortion
Rape
Trafficking
Slavery

Picking off individuals
One at a time
Once they're in
They'll never get out

Escape is what they want
But for escape you need to speak out
Speaking out gets you slaughtered

Hence why evil continues

Stopping something requires the
acknowledgement of its existence
You can't acknowledge what you can't talk
about
Victims are muted for fear of retribution
Onlookers are wilfully ignorant for fear of
inconvenience
Perpetrators are smug for knowing this will
continue

The power of silence
Speaking out subverts it
Subverting it stops evil

Overcome the Offended Feelings

Disagree with ideology
Disagree with rules
Disagree with approved standards
Disagree with anything

Like a furious volcano
Watch the outrage explode
Good luck escaping with your life
For they want you life over

Everything has its time in the spotlight
Every fad
Every conspiracy
Every maypole to dance around
It will be latched onto by society

Refuse to dance
Refuse to agree
Rest in peace

Why do we do this?
So much aggression over belief
They're supposed to make us better
We use them as excuses to be terrible

When someone disagrees
If you slaughter them
Is your belief worth it?
Endless cancellation to preserve your
insecurities

Cancelling destroys
Cancelling desolates
Why not just disengage?

If someone disagrees
Let them go
Let yourself move on
So much freedom
So much respect

Being offended is ok
Being a decent human being is better

A Game of Blame

All of us humans
Flaws aplenty
As many faults as there are people

You're crabby, aren't you?
"It's because I'm a Taurus"
"The alignment of stars messes with me"
"Neptune's ascension ascends my rage"

Why are you blaming the planets?
What have the stars got to do with your
petulance?
Did your date of birth predispose your furious
nature?

You're such a stress head
"I get that from my Dad"
"It runs in the family"
"My parents gave me my anxious nature"

Did they literally give it to you?
Did they gift wrap your anxiety?
Were you pleased when you opened it?
Did you put it on your mantlepiece?
Do you keep it in your pocket?

Your tone is very aggressive
"I had a bad childhood"
"I came from a broken home"
"My parents were always fighting"
"It's all I've ever known"

All you've ever known?
Could you not learn anything else?
Have you tried everything?
Is passing the torch of the fight acceptable?

Being treated like scum
Does it justify treating others the same?
A genetic history
Is it impossible to manage?
Star signs and astrology
Does that make it ok to be a brat?

Character traits
Good and bad
They're like pets
There to be managed or allowed to run amok
Kept in check or permitted to destroy everything

Give them boundaries
Or they'll give you hell

The Stigma Won't Stop Us

So many problems in life
Why are they so mysterious?

It's because we don't talk about them

Nervous breakdowns
Self-harm
Disordered eating
Suicidal behaviour

Ask your mates if they're ok
It gets brushed off
Turned into a joke
Swept under the carpet
Treated like an inconvenience
Accused of being unmanly

Problems of the mind
Ignoring isn't solving
It's prolonging and enabling

The plights of all women
Biological processes
Daily harassment
Attacked and murdered

Subjugation through history

Ask men
They clam up
Crack wise
Refuse to see
Unable to conceive (in any way)

Stigmas
Obstacles to solutions for problems
Challenging but not impossible
They can be overcome

Use your voice
Have the conversation
Temporary discomfort lead to permanent
benefits

Don't let the stigmas win the battle

Get Me Offline

Buttons, beeps and bing-bongs
Messages sent and received
Endless consumables demanding consumption
Too many tasks demanding immediate attention

"Being online makes your life better"

It doesn't feel better
It feels tiring
It feels stressful
It feels overwhelming

Step away from the web
For a week
For a day
For an hour
See the difference?

Peace and quiet
Thinking my own thoughts
Freedom from being pursued

Take a moment to wonder
Who's pursuing us?

People who need us
People who like us
People who want us

Why?
Why indeed

They want your money
They want your soul
They want your body
They want your identity

Don't give them control
Reliance on the internet is what they want
Salvage some independence
You won't regret it

One Voice For All

Several social sub-strata
Standing for different causes

Upholding the traditional order
Rebelling against it
Uncovering conspiracies
Disproving them
Creating new innovations
Discouraging their pursuits

Endless differences
One similarity

Each group has its leaders

They use their voices
They incite the actions
They preach the manifestos
They lead by example

The followers?
They lap it up

Nodding in agreement
Conspiratorial glances and winks

Reckoning they're the best group
Because their figurehead tells them so

Wouldn't it be interesting
If they thought for themselves?
Wouldn't it be interesting
If they took a look at the world?
Wouldn't it be interesting
If they made their own decisions?

As long as their leaders are on hand
They won't bother
Their thinking is done for them
One voice covers them all

9 789358 736359